LOVE **SUNG**

31 DAYS TO DISCOVER
YOUR TRUE IDENTITY

Theron Hatch

Scripture references and permission information.

Published in Nashville, Tennessee by Love Sung, LLC

ISBN: 1523621605
ISBN-13: 978-1523621606

For Mary, Kate, Anna, and Luke.
Your melodies and harmonies inspire me.

THERON **HATCH**

FOREWORD

Every one of us is gifted, and the world is in need of our gifts to be known, grown, and shown. Theron shared the beautiful idea about *Love Sung* while he and I talked one evening on my back porch. I had seen his care for others that had grown from the rediscovery of his own "song". When he talked about how the idea came to be, the experiences and story that led to the willingness to express his own song, I urged him to just do it. We are made to dream, think, and do. I have seen that when we do, we ourselves are blessed by the creativity and the risk involved as we press forward. And I have also seen that others, those who are listening, are also inspired to step into their own gifts and risks. Theron's *Love Sung* is as much his story as it is the story of anyone of us who has put our song away, thinking it didn't matter, only to one day realize that something important is missing. That the symphony is incomplete without us taking our seat in the orchestra. I hope that you will hear the words in Theron's offering as purely as I know he presents them.

Chip Dodd, PhD
Founder and Director, The Center for Professional Excellence
Author of *The Voice of the Heart*

NOTE TO THE READER

This is the second edition of this book. The only change from the first edition is the inclusion of journal pages for each day. The first edition didn't have any room for notes. *Love Sung* was designed to be read as a daily devotional. It contains 31 identity topics. However, some readers of my early drafts and first edition found it difficult to put it down after reading the first topic... or the second... or the third. In fact, I think many read right through it to the end on the very first time through. So if you find yourself wanting to read through it all in one sitting, that's ok. I want to encourage you to stop and take note of any topics that you sense may require some additional marinating. Before you begin each day, be sure to have something to write with and be willing to listen. Revelations will come. When they do, allow the Holy Spirit to teach you and perhaps heal you of any misunderstandings of who you are in Christ. You may find you have to go back again and again to really understand why a particular topic keeps hanging around. Some of these truths have been my sparring companions for weeks, months, and even years, always revealing more about myself and the things I've struggled to bring to the Light.

My hope and prayer is that several of these topics will present you with a fresh perspective on your identity in Christ. The right hand page of each daily topic is a lined page for journaling with a corresponding question to prompt your thinking. If a particular topic has challenged you to dig deeper, or maybe revealed a wound from your past, or even affirmed a recovered area of your life, take a moment to journal what you are hearing about who you truly are. Don't be overwhelmed with the notion of journaling. It's nothing more than just simply recording what you hear as you read and listen.

Finally, an important step in the process of learning something new about yourself is having the courage to share what you've learned with another close and trusted friend. This can bring healing and is how we become truly known to one another. You are likely to have experiences that others can relate to and learn from (and vice versa).

Enjoy the book. I enjoyed writing it, though a part of me wishes I didn't have to.

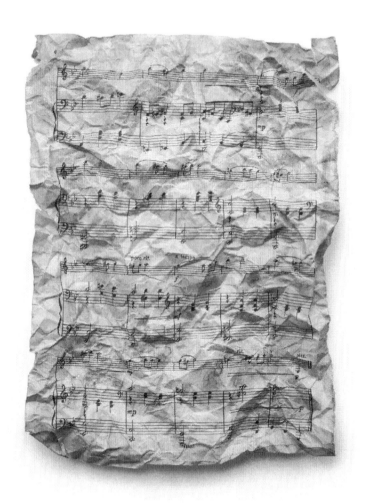

INTRODUCTION

Most of the time life teaches us quietly and slowly. We learn through seasons of waiting. Every once in a while, though, God speaks through moments of clarity. The truth in this devotional came to me in several such moments.

My first glimpse came during a symphony rehearsal. The orchestra was reading through a new composition written specifically for it. It was the first time the piece had been played and the composer was there to provide some guidance for both the conductor and the musicians. I was playing bass, but the composition did not have a bass part during the opening movements. As the conductor gave the downbeat and the orchestra began to play, I found myself mesmerized watching the composer as he was listening to his creation draw its first breath. I remember seeing his expressions as the melodies and harmonies played out. What was he experiencing? Did the orchestra capture the essence of what he had intended? Were the nuances and intensities living up to what began as just an idea in his head? I saw a smile at times, and also witnessed an occasional wince as a note was missed or played in the wrong key. A thought came to me. I pictured God like that composer. He has written great symphonies for us to participate in, calling each of us to sing or play out our part. For it to sound good, we really have to be practiced and engaged fully in the music. Are we playing the part we are called to play? Are we playing it well and in harmony with others? It was a simple picture, but that picture would stick with me for a while and I couldn't let it go. That was the first moment of clarity.

A short time later, I played bass with a mission team of big band musicians in Glasgow, Scotland. We ministered to local churches in and around that city by playing big band concerts, spreading joy to a city and country that seemed to have lost some of its rich Christian heritage. During our concerts we shared the gospel through our personal stories of redemption. As I prepared to share my testimony at one such concert, God brought the composer story back to me with a force and clarity that could only be from Him. He wanted me to tell the truth of my story, one that I'd been hiding.

He had given me a song to sing and I hadn't been singing it.

This was my second moment of clarity. I knew that my song represented my identity. As I was sharing my story that night, I took a sheet of paper from my music stand, crumpled it before the audience, and threw it to the floor. What was on that crumpled sheet represented what God had composed for me to sing, my identity expressing something unique… and I had rejected it.

I'd thrown it away.

My song.

My personal, God-given song.

I'd become disgusted with my true identity and refused to claim it.

Throughout my life, and especially in my earlier years, my song was liked and disliked, accepted and rejected, twisted, manipulated, and distorted. Standing in front of the crowd in Scotland that evening, I realized that no matter what it's been through and even how it's been received, it was still *my* song. I had a choice to make, but the choice was surprisingly easy.

I wanted to learn to sing it again. I had to learn to sing it again. I had to claim it as mine.

But in order to recover it, I had to get in tune with its composer. Christ held the key to the tune, because he is the source of my identity - the restorer of God's image in me. I picked up the crumpled paper and smoothed it out on my music stand again.

God has been unpacking these truths through the usual slow and quiet process His Holy Spirit is so good at. My prayer is that He does the same for you. When you discover your true identity and begin walking in it, you will begin to hear Love sung through you.

Theron Hatch, January 2016

LOVE SUNG

Your journey begins now...

- Day 1 -

YOUR SONG
IS UNIQUE.

God composes.

He creates.

He loves beauty and is a master craftsman.

He is intentional.

You are a result of His careful planning.

A chair in His orchestra
has your name on it.

FOR WE ARE GOD'S MASTERPIECE. HE HAS CREATED US ANEW IN
CHRIST JESUS, SO WE CAN DO THE GOOD THINGS HE PLANNED
FOR US LONG AGO. **EPHESIANS 2:10 (NLT)**

How are you unique?

_____

_____

_____

_____

_____

_____

_____

_____

_____

_____

_____

_____

_____

_____

_____

_____

_____

_____

_____

– Day 2 –

YOUR **SONG** EXPRESSES YOUR **IDENTITY** WITHOUT **LIMITING** YOU.

Your song expresses the true nature of how God made you.

It represents you in your relationship with others, but doesn't solely define you.

Through your song, others will get the opportunity to know the entirety of who you are.

What does knowing your true identity mean to you?

_____

_____

_____

_____

_____

_____

_____

_____

_____

_____

_____

_____

_____

_____

_____

_____

_____

_____

– Day 3 –

YOUR GOD-GIVEN **SONG** HAS A **PURPOSE** ROOTED IN **CREATION**.

God doesn't make mistakes.

He is purposeful and intentional in His designs.

You have purpose because you are His creation.

Your song reveals God's nature, His eternal plan. His greater purpose uses your song as nothing else can.

Your song is a gift for you and others.

EVERY GOOD AND PERFECT GIFT IS FROM ABOVE, COMING DOWN FROM THE FATHER OF THE HEAVENLY LIGHTS, WHO DOES NOT CHANGE LIKE SHIFTING SHADOWS. **JAMES 1:17 (NIV)**

How does seeing a divine purpose change your thinking?

_____

_____

_____

_____

_____

_____

_____

_____

_____

_____

_____

_____

_____

_____

_____

_____

_____

_____

– Day 4 –

YOUR **SONG** ECHOES **BEAUTIFUL** **MUSIC** TO ITS **CREATOR** AND TO THOSE **AROUND** YOU.

We are enraptured when we see a snow-capped mountain peak. The awesome power of a crashing wave stops us in our tracks.

But nothing compares to the sublimity of God's human instrument singing the Master's song.

God composed your song to reveal His beauty.

Sing! The world will stop and take notice.

HE PUT A NEW SONG IN MY MOUTH, A HYMN OF PRAISE TO OUR GOD. MANY WILL SEE AND FEAR THE LORD AND PUT THEIR TRUST IN HIM. **PSALMS 40:3 (NIV)**

How do you respond to God's beauty in you?

_____
_____
_____
_____
_____
_____
_____
_____
_____
_____
_____
_____
_____
_____
_____
_____
_____

– Day 5 –

SOME MAY **SHUT** THEIR **EARS** TO YOUR SONG. KEEP **SINGING** EVEN WHEN YOU FEEL **NOBODY** WANTS TO **HEAR**.

Rejection by those closest to you hurts. Don't allow the wounds to change your song.

Pain can open a rich awareness of your own depth and add resonance to your song.

Lean into the pain of rejection and sing from the depths of your soul.

YOU'RE GOING TO FIND THAT THERE WILL BE TIMES WHEN PEOPLE WILL HAVE NO STOMACH FOR SOLID TEACHING, BUT WILL FILL UP ON SPIRITUAL JUNK FOOD-CATCHY OPINIONS THAT TICKLE THEIR FANCY. THEY'LL TURN THEIR BACKS ON TRUTH AND CHASE MIRAGES. BUT YOU-KEEP YOUR EYE ON WHAT YOU'RE DOING; ACCEPT THE HARD TIMES ALONG WITH THE GOOD; KEEP THE MESSAGE ALIVE; DO A THOROUGH JOB AS GOD'S SERVANT. **2 TIMOTHY 4:3-5 (THE MESSAGE)**

Why is rejection so painful? How did Jesus handle it?

_____

_____

_____

_____

_____

_____

_____

_____

_____

_____

_____

_____

_____

_____

_____

_____

_____

_____

– Day 6 –

SOME WILL **APPRECIATE** AND **VALUE** YOUR **SONG.** SOME WILL **NOT.** APPLAUSE IS NOT YOUR **GOAL.**

You will face rejection because you have a sworn enemy.

The darkness hates your song because it reminds others of where the light is.

Despite the rejection, you must choose to sing out the truth of who you are.

Acceptance from others may not come, but your heart will be filled.

𝄋

FOR AM I NOW SEEKING THE FAVOR OF MEN, OR OF GOD? OR AM I STRIVING TO PLEASE MEN? IF I WERE STILL TRYING TO PLEASE MEN, I WOULD NOT BE A BOND-SERVANT OF CHRIST.
GALATIANS 1:10 (NASB)

Where are you seeking applause instead of living out
God's purposes in your life?

_____

_____

_____

_____

_____

_____

_____

_____

_____

_____

_____

_____

_____

_____

_____

– Day 7 –

SOME WILL TRY TO CONVINCE YOU TO SING A DIFFERENT SONG. DON'T GIVE IN. CONTINUE TO SING YOUR SONG.

Your song may intimidate others because some despise their own song.

The beauty of your song may be painful to those who have rejected Beauty and the Creator.

Be true to God with what is yours and continue to sing out.

THEN HE SAID TO THE DISCIPLES, "ANYONE WHO ACCEPTS YOUR MESSAGE IS ALSO ACCEPTING ME. AND ANYONE WHO REJECTS YOU IS REJECTING ME. AND ANYONE WHO REJECTS ME IS REJECTING GOD, WHO SENT ME." **LUKE 10:16 (NLT)**

What challenges have kept you from walking in integrity?

_____

_____

_____

_____

_____

_____

_____

_____

_____

_____

_____

_____

_____

_____

_____

_____

_____

– Day 8 –

IF YOU **CANNOT** HEAR YOUR SONG, IT IS **NOT LOST**. FIND SOMEWHERE **QUIET**. REDISCOVER IT. THE MUSIC MAY TAKE SOME **TIME**, BUT DON'T GIVE UP.

Life can overwhelm us and cause hearing loss. The daily routine is often like listening to a radio with a jack-hammer in the room. When you get home at the end of a long day, the dull ache of the machinery just won't go away.

Spend time in quiet and peaceful places. The quiet will clear the residue of noise and restore your peace.

When you quiet your heart, what do you hear?

_____
_____
_____
_____
_____
_____
_____
_____
_____
_____
_____
_____
_____
_____
_____
_____
_____
_____
_____

– Day 9 –

AS YOU **SING**, YOU'LL BEGIN TO HEAR **OTHER** MELODIES **AROUND** YOU. YOU AREN'T **OUT** OF TUNE. YOU ARE JUST **LEARNING** TO **HARMONIZE**.

As relational creatures, we crave experiences with others. Intentionally seeking relationship requires you to sing out your own song. It's a vulnerable experience, because you will always risk rejection. Stay in the vulnerability and sing.

The Composer has made your song to be harmonious with others. Keep singing and you will eventually hear others sing in harmony with you.

Harmonize, don't compromise.

TO SUM UP, ALL OF YOU BE HARMONIOUS, SYMPATHETIC, BROTHERLY, KINDHEARTED, AND HUMBLE IN SPIRIT;
1 PETER 3:8 (NASB)

Who truly knows you? Why did you choose them?

– Day 10 –

YOUR **SONG** HAS **POWER...** EVEN THE POWER OF **LIFE** AND **DEATH**. SING FOR **LIFE**.

Something powerful exists in the spoken word; in the utterances that come out of your mouth.

The antagonist of your soul rearranges songs, bringing discord and death.

The Composer spoke life into being. He conquered death with a word.

Sing the song He gave you, and you will see life bloom all around.

Which of your words cause others to smile?

_____

_____

_____

_____

_____

_____

_____

_____

_____

_____

_____

_____

_____

_____

_____

_____

_____

_____

– Day 11 –

IN MUSIC, A **REST** HAS AS MUCH **VALUE** AS A **NOTE** PLAYED. MAKE SURE YOU TAKE **TIME** TO **QUIET** YOURSELF TO KEEP IN **STEP** WITH GOD'S **RHYTHM.**

A musical rest gives distinction and emphasis to your notes.

It maintains rhythm and flow.

Finding rest in the midst of chaos is significant to the quality of your song.

Without regular rest your song is rushed and unbalanced.

THEN JESUS SAID, "LET'S GO OFF BY OURSELVES TO A QUIET PLACE AND REST AWHILE." **MARK 6:31 (NLT)**

How do you rest?

_____

_____

_____

_____

_____

_____

_____

_____

_____

_____

_____

_____

_____

_____

_____

_____

_____

_____

– Day 12 –

WHEN YOU ARE **UNSURE** OF **WHAT** TO **SING** OR **WHERE** TO **SING, ASK!**

There is no greater joy than having these questions answered.

God is a relational being, and he delights in conversation with His friends.

He gave us the Holy Spirit for this very purpose.

When we ask Him for help, he listens and responds!

BUT WHEN HE, THE SPIRIT OF TRUTH, COMES, HE WILL GUIDE YOU INTO ALL THE TRUTH. HE WILL NOT SPEAK ON HIS OWN; HE WILL SPEAK ONLY WHAT HE HEARS, AND HE WILL TELL YOU WHAT IS YET TO COME. **JOHN** 16:13 **(NIV)**

Do you ask for help when needed? Why or why not?

_____

_____

_____

_____

_____

_____

_____

_____

_____

_____

_____

_____

_____

_____

_____

_____

_____

_____

– Day 13 –

DO NOT **ALTER** YOUR **SONG** IN THE NAME OF **LOVE**. YOUR SONG IS LOVE **EXPRESSED**.

Worship God by singing the song
He gave you in the first place.

If you will love others with your words and
your deeds, while always keeping your voice
strong and steady, you will fully
demonstrate the love of God.

This is true worship.

This is your love song.

I PRAY THAT YOUR LOVE WILL OVERFLOW MORE AND MORE,
AND THAT YOU WILL KEEP ON GROWING IN KNOWLEDGE AND
UNDERSTANDING. FOR I WANT YOU TO UNDERSTAND WHAT
REALLY MATTERS, SO THAT YOU MAY LIVE PURE AND BLAMELESS
LIVES UNTIL THE DAY OF CHRIST'S RETURN.
PHILIPPIANS 1:9-10 (NLT)

How do you respond when you can't make others happy?

_____

_____

_____

_____

_____

_____

_____

_____

_____

_____

_____

_____

_____

_____

_____

_____

_____

_____

_____

– Day 14 –

MANY **STAGES, CONCERT** HALLS, STREET **CORNERS** AND **REMOTE** FIELDS EXIST WHERE YOU COULD SING. FIND WHAT IS **BEST** FOR YOU. LET **GOD** BE YOUR **GUIDE.**

God will show you many opportunities, both large and small, to share your song.

Don't worry about what the opportunity looks like. Your song is made for where God places you.

Don't despise where you are placed.

Sometimes small venues have the biggest impact.

VERY TRULY I TELL YOU, WHOEVER BELIEVES IN ME WILL DO THE WORKS I HAVE BEEN DOING, AND THEY WILL DO EVEN GREATER THINGS THAN THESE, BECAUSE I AM GOING TO THE FATHER.
JOHN 14:12 (NIV)

How can you impact the people around you right now?

_____

_____

_____

_____

_____

_____

_____

_____

_____

_____

_____

_____

_____

_____

_____

_____

_____

_____

– Day 15 –

BE **PASSIONATE**, **NOT PUSHY!** SHARE YOUR **SONG** WITH DESIRE, BUT WITHOUT **DEMAND.**

It's good and natural to want to share your song; just don't demand an audience.

Likewise, if you keep your song to yourself, how will anyone hear and know you?

Give your song away to others without expectation. Engage fully in the relationships that God gives you by becoming known.

One day you may hear those closest to you humming your song.

HOW, THEN, CAN THEY CALL ON THE ONE THEY HAVE NOT
BELIEVED IN? AND HOW CAN THEY BELIEVE IN THE ONE OF
WHOM THEY HAVE NOT HEARD? AND HOW CAN THEY HEAR
WITHOUT SOMEONE PREACHING TO THEM? AND HOW CAN
ANYONE PREACH UNLESS THEY ARE SENT? AS IT IS WRITTEN:
"HOW BEAUTIFUL ARE THE FEET OF THOSE WHO BRING GOOD
NEWS!" **ROMANS 10:14-15 (NIV)**

What do others like about you?

_____

_____

_____

_____

_____

_____

_____

_____

_____

_____

_____

_____

_____

_____

_____

_____

_____

_____

- Day 16 -

YOUR SONG IS BEAUTIFUL.

God is beauty and His creation reflects that beauty. You were made in the image of God, and your song expresses that image.

What the world calls beauty doesn't define you. Your temporary physical nature does not reflect who you truly are. Don't let false concepts of beauty cheapen your appreciation for God's creation. You are an eternal reflection of Ultimate Beauty.

Love your song.

Sing your song.

AND WE ALL, WHO WITH UNVEILED FACES CONTEMPLATE THE LORD'S GLORY, ARE BEING TRANSFORMED INTO HIS IMAGE WITH EVER-INCREASING GLORY, WHICH COMES FROM THE LORD, WHO IS THE SPIRIT. **2 CORINTHIANS 3:18 (NIV)**

LOVE **SUNG**

Where is God's beauty reflected in your life?

_____

_____

_____

_____

_____

_____

_____

_____

_____

_____

_____

_____

_____

_____

_____

_____

_____

_____

– Day 17 –

SING **WITH** CLARITY!

Pursue purity!

When there is a disconnect between the beauty of your song and the way you live your life, you diminish your offering.

Keep your voice pure, so your song will go out unhindered.

EVEN BEFORE HE MADE THE WORLD, GOD LOVED US AND CHOSE US IN CHRIST TO BE HOLY AND WITHOUT FAULT IN HIS EYES.
EPHESIANS 1:4 (NLT)

What things are you keeping from God?

_____

_____

_____

_____

_____

_____

_____

_____

_____

_____

_____

_____

_____

_____

_____

_____

_____

– Day 18 –

TRUST THE MAKER OF THE MUSIC AND THE PART HE CALLS YOU TO PLAY.

Trusting another being with our very life is one of the most difficult aspects of being human. When you trust another (even God himself) with the deepest part of who you are, you become vulnerable and exposed. It's a process of giving up control and allowing God to guide you into your true identity.

When you are scared and feel alone, cry out to God with your song of praise to him.

He will not leave you or forsake you. He loves to hear you sing.

BE STRONG AND COURAGEOUS. DO NOT BE AFRAID OR TERRIFIED BECAUSE OF THEM, FOR THE LORD YOUR GOD GOES WITH YOU; HE WILL NEVER LEAVE YOU NOR FORSAKE YOU.
DEUTERONOMY 31:6 (NIV)

Why is trusting God so hard?

_____

_____

_____

_____

_____

_____

_____

_____

_____

_____

_____

_____

_____

_____

_____

_____

_____

_____

– Day 19 –

LISTEN FOR THE MELODY AND FEEL THE MOTION OF GOD'S RHYTHM WITHIN.

There will be times for following the music written on the page and other times for improvisation.

When we walk in our identity, we experience the thrill of true freedom.

Don't let that freedom lead you astray though.

God will protect you with spiritual guardrails.

Pay attention.

IT IS FOR FREEDOM THAT CHRIST HAS SET US FREE. STAND FIRM, THEN, AND DO NOT LET YOURSELVES BE BURDENED AGAIN BY A YOKE OF SLAVERY. **GALATIANS 5:1 (NIV)**

Are you a good listener? What do you receive from it?

_____

_____

_____

_____

_____

_____

_____

_____

_____

_____

_____

_____

_____

_____

_____

_____

_____

_____

– *Day 20* –

WHEN YOUR **SONG** IS IN HARMONY WITH THE SONGS OF OTHERS, SING OUT AND **MARVEL** AT THE **BEAUTY CREATED** BY GOD'S **MELODIES** JOINING TOGETHER.

Just like a solo, singing harmonies with others is a rewarding experience and it brings out a different sound altogether.

During these opportunities, listen and blend, knowing that together something special is happening.

God is building up His church.

What do you do to keep your relationships strong?

_____

_____

_____

_____

_____

_____

_____

_____

_____

_____

_____

_____

_____

_____

_____

_____

_____

– Day 21 –

THERE WILL BE **TIMES** WHEN YOUR **SONG** REQUIRES A **SOLO PERFORMANCE.**

SING **BOLDLY!**

Singing your song publicly is scary... at first. Failure and possible embarrassment loom large.

Remember that God himself has already declared your song beautiful, and His declarations are true.

When he calls you to sing out, access His power within you to sing out boldly.

AND MY MESSAGE AND MY PREACHING WERE NOT IN PERSUASIVE WORDS OF WISDOM, BUT IN DEMONSTRATION OF THE SPIRIT AND OF POWER, SO THAT YOUR FAITH WOULD NOT REST ON THE WISDOM OF MEN, BUT ON THE POWER OF GOD.
1 CORINTHIANS 2:4-5 (NASB)

Do you fear being the real you? Why or why not?

_____

_____

_____

_____

_____

_____

_____

_____

_____

_____

_____

_____

_____

_____

_____

_____

_____

– Day 22 –

YOUR **SONG** MUST BE **LISTENED** FOR AND **LEARNED** FROM. GET TO **KNOW** AND BE **COMFORTABLE** WITH YOUR OWN **VOICE!**

Though your song is inside you when you are born, recognizing it is not always easy. It takes time to learn the sound and melody of your song.

Singing it beautifully requires that you love who you are enough to let others hear it, and hear it over and over again.

Continue to wrestle with this vulnerability and you'll begin to experience peace.

What can you learn from how God made you?

_____
_____
_____
_____
_____
_____
_____
_____
_____
_____
_____
_____
_____
_____
_____
_____
_____

– Day 23 –

YOUR **SONG** IS BORN INTO A **WORLD** FILLED WITH **NOISE.** SOUNDS ARE **DISTORTED** AND YOUR SONG **BEGINS** IN **CONFUSION.** SING OUT AND LET GOD **TUNE** YOUR **VOICE!**

The tragedy of sin that occurred in the Garden of Eden separated us from God. Anything attempted without Him is incomplete and tainted, because it is accomplished by self.

Your song cries out to its Creator to make it whole and to give it purpose.

It is through our song that we confess our need for Jesus to save and restore us.

What are the clues that you are trying to control your life?

_____

_____

_____

_____

_____

_____

_____

_____

_____

_____

_____

_____

_____

_____

_____

_____

_____

_____

– Day 24 –

THERE WILL BE TIMES WHEN YOUR **SONG** WILL SOUND **OLD** AND **OUTDATED**. IT IS **NOT** AND **NEVER** WILL BE.

Hearing your own voice over and over may begin to sound boring, especially when you hear something new elsewhere.

You may be tempted to find more relevance by changing your sound because new seems exciting. Don't confuse shiny and new with being renewed.

Each new day presents an opportunity to be reminded of why you sing and why your song is so important.

BECAUSE OF THE LORD'S GREAT LOVE WE ARE NOT CONSUMED, FOR HIS COMPASSIONS NEVER FAIL. THEY ARE NEW EVERY MORNING; GREAT IS YOUR FAITHFULNESS.
LAMENTATIONS 3:22-23 (NIV)

How are you renewing your mind in truth?

_____

_____

_____

_____

_____

_____

_____

_____

_____

_____

_____

_____

_____

_____

_____

_____

_____

– Day 25 –

THERE WILL BE **TIMES** WHEN YOUR **SONG FRUSTRATES** YOU, AND YOU **FEEL** LIKE IT'S **HOLDING** YOU BACK. THIS IS A **NORMAL** RESPONSE.

You'll think your song doesn't matter because you've been singing it for so long and not getting any traction.

You may consider options on how you can make it better or more appealing, because you're sensing that you don't have anything to offer anyone anymore.
This is simply not true.

Don't change your song. Someone is listening and needs to hear it.

How can God restore you from frustration or defeat?

_____

_____

_____

_____

_____

_____

_____

_____

_____

_____

_____

_____

_____

_____

_____

_____

_____

– Day 26 –

SOME WILL TRY TO **BORROW** YOUR **SONG** AND **SELL** IT AS **THEIR** OWN. BUT **FEAR NOT...** IT IS **DESIGNED** TO BE SUNG BY **YOU** ONLY.

To some, your song will be so beautiful that all they see is dollar signs and personal recognition for themselves.

It may even be appealing to you to stand in the spotlight, but don't sell out.

Sing out!

Are you *free* to respond to God's call for *your own life?*

_____

_____

_____

_____

_____

_____

_____

_____

_____

_____

_____

_____

_____

_____

_____

_____

_____

- Day 27 -

SOME WILL **ATTEMPT** TO **ALTER** YOUR **SONG** FOR **UNINTENDED** PURPOSES.

The temptation to compromise for the sake of agreement is strong, but it never works.

You can't harmonize when you are singing out of tune!

The result is loss of identity and a process of morphing into a new man-made creature.

When you are comfortable saying no to conceding your identity to another, you will experience your own song in its fullness.

BUT ABOVE ALL, MY BRETHREN, DO NOT SWEAR, EITHER BY HEAVEN OR BY EARTH OR WITH ANY OTHER OATH; BUT YOUR YES IS TO BE YES, AND YOUR NO, NO, SO THAT YOU MAY NOT FALL UNDER JUDGMENT. **JAMES 5:12 (NIV)**

Are you trying to change your identity?

_____

_____

_____

_____

_____

_____

_____

_____

_____

_____

_____

_____

_____

_____

_____

_____

_____

– Day 28 –

GOD IS THE **AUTHOR** OF YOUR SONG AND IT IS FOR HIS ORCHESTRATION THAT YOU WERE **CREATED**. BRING IT CONFIDENTLY TO THE **STAGE**.

God designed you to be part of something that is bigger than you, but still requires all of you. You matter. You have significance.

It would be noticeable if you were missing. His symphony would be incomplete without you.

Be fully you, intentionally engaged in relationships with God and others. This is the Church.

HE MAKES THE WHOLE BODY FIT TOGETHER PERFECTLY. AS EACH PART DOES ITS OWN SPECIAL WORK, IT HELPS THE OTHER PARTS GROW, SO THAT THE WHOLE BODY IS HEALTHY AND GROWING AND FULL OF LOVE. **EPHESIANS 4:16 (NLT)**

Who do you miss most when they aren't around? Why?

_____

_____

_____

_____

_____

_____

_____

_____

_____

_____

_____

_____

_____

_____

_____

_____

– Day 29 –

YOUR **SONG** IS THE **CRY** OF YOUR **HEART** TO BE **KNOWN** AND TO BE IN **RELATIONSHIP.**

We reach out from our very first breath seeking relationship with others. Our song tells others who we are.

We were never intended to live alone or to hide our song from others. When we isolate, we slowly die and our song grows weak.

Sing out your song daily. Give others an opportunity to hear it so they can know you... the real you.

I WAITED PATIENTLY FOR THE LORD; HE TURNED TO ME AND HEARD MY CRY. **PSALMS 40:1 (NIV)**

Is it uncomfortable letting others in? Why or why not?

_____

_____

_____

_____

_____

_____

_____

_____

_____

_____

_____

_____

_____

_____

_____

_____

— Day 30 —

WE HAVE AT ANY MOMENT'S NOTICE THE **BEST MUSIC TEACHER** AND FRIEND **AVAILABLE** FOR **GUIDANCE IN TEMPO** AND **RHYTHM.**

We are given the Holy Spirit to speak the truth of God's call on our life.

Our song is a reflection of this communication.

The Spirit of God works with us daily, keeping us in beat with God's eternal rhythm.

When we feel lost or out of step, we simply must connect with the rhythm of God He has placed in us by His Holy Spirit.

HE WILL GLORIFY ME BECAUSE IT IS FROM ME THAT HE WILL RECEIVE WHAT HE WILL MAKE KNOWN TO YOU. **JOHN 16:14 (NIV)**

What is the Holy Spirit trying to teach you today?

– Day 31 –

YOUR **SONG** IS **GOOD** BECAUSE IT IS **GOD'S FIRST.**

When your song is surrendered to the leading of the Holy Spirit, its melody expresses God's deep and abiding love to all who hear it.

Our song becomes a gift to those who will listen, as if Jesus were speaking in person.

When we give up control and allow God to work through us, those we come in contact with will see a real and unhindered view of Christ in us.

BY THIS EVERYONE WILL KNOW THAT YOU ARE MY DISCIPLES, IF YOU LOVE ONE ANOTHER. **JOHN 13:35 (NIV)**

In what way is your life a gift to you, to others, to God?

THERON **HATCH**

ACKNOWLEDGEMENTS

I owe a great deal of thanks to so many people who have walked this journey with me.

Chip Dodd, you started me on this journey of rediscovery of my song. *The Voice of the Heart* book changed my life and I treasure your friendship and encouragement.

Ken Davis, thank you for your humor, friendship, and willingness to mentor me over the years, including pushing me to finish a triathlon. We were connected for a purpose. I am forever grateful.

Austin Cagle, your finesse as my editor helped me finish this book with excellence. You took my vision and we created something beautiful. I value your friendship. Your own song inspires me.

Paul Smith and Derek Faulkner, you have been my steady companions and truth-tellers these past few years. Not once did you plug your ears when I sang my song. Thanks for reminding me that it is good. I love you both and can't wait for Thursday.

Bill Rawnsley, our first meeting at a Starbucks was by no means an accident. You've seen me at some of my lowest and watched me climb out of deep ditches of my own creation. Thanks for believing in me enough to speak truth into my life. I'm seeing your own song emerge beautifully and many are listening to it.

John Scott Evans, it all began sitting next to each other in the FBA orchestra. You always told me my song was special, but I didn't really know what you meant until I started living what's in this book. You showed me what it means to be a courageous musician.

Camp Kirkland, you invited me into a world of music and missions. It was one such mission trip with you and a symphony you selflessly lead that inspired the truths found in this book.

Randi Bivens, you showed me my song was good by trusting me with your own song. I'm thankful for your friendship. It's a joy playing with you each Sunday in our dynamic duo rhythm section.

Tara Daniel, thank you for your time, honesty, and wisdom with *Love Sung's* early drafts and revisions. Your insight is so appreciated. Your friendship more so. Thanks for keeping our family healthy and strong.

Mike Stalnaker and Scott Little, you've built a great company and continue to lead it well. Thank you both for investing in me.

Belle Aire CR team, you guys rock. Thank you for giving me a place to experience freedom and learn about my song.

To the guys at RLMO, you gave me an opportunity to learn by teaching. You men who daily must choose to stay in the pain to see the healing come, I applaud you. It's my honor to call you friends.

To my friends at VCC, you were a hospital for a wounded veteran of the faith. You provided a safe place to heal, grow, and learn how to sing again. Literally. Thank you from the bottom of my healed heart.

To the faculty and staff at PCA, you do an incredible work for the Lord in training up a new generation of bold believers. You are that picture of an orchestra. My kids have learned not only how to harmonize with others, but also to boldly sing out their own song.

Mom and Dad, you have supported me and our family always. Thank you for being a great example of Godly parents and great mentors to so many. And for not giving up on me.

Lindsay, Heidi, Jon, JoJo, and your respective spouses and kids have blessed me more than you'll know, and more than just because you're my siblings. I'm hearing your own songs spring forth in a majestic tribute to our Creator.

Luke, some say that I helped you in your time of need. That may be true. But without you coming into our family, I would not be who I am today. God told me He has a special plan for your life. Listen for His voice and your song within as you grow. I will too.

Anna, the piano was made for you. I've enjoyed watching you grow as a musician and writer. You have a wonderful song to sing out. The world has not heard it fully yet, but it will in time.

Kate, I've watched you face and overcome challenges in your life thus far as you've actively listened for your own song. You continue to amaze me with your desire for excellence and your maturity in your faith. Keep singing your beautiful song.

Mary, thanks for not giving up on me. Deep wounds, especially the ones that take many applications of ointment and bandages, are painful and often take extra time to heal. You gave me time and loved me through it. Thank you. I love you.

Jesus, you saved me. Thank you. My song is for you.

ABOUT THE AUTHOR

It's no accident that Theron Hatch would write a book about music and song. He's been playing one of several instruments since elementary school, writing songs since middle school, and traveling with these gifts around the world, even into the present day. It all began with trumpet lessons and later switching to electric bass, guitar, and piano. A love of writing and teaching, with an inspired imagination, fueled this work.

Theron is a published author, songwriter, bass, guitar, and piano player, and sings and leads worship at his church in Murfreesboro, TN. He is surrounded by a musical family. His wife Mary, daughters Kate and Anna, and son Luke keep his house filled with beautiful melodies.

If you've been impacted by this book, please let Theron know through one of the contact methods below. Your reviews are also very important and appreciated, especially for a newly published author. Please take a moment and consider writing a thoughtful review of *Love Sung* at Amazon. Join the Love Sung newsletter to receive updates and new *Love Sung* material by visiting lovesungbook.com.

Contact info:
Love Sung, LLC
PO Box 11661
Murfreesboro, TN 37129
Email: books@lovesung.co
Book Website: lovesungbook.com
Author Website: theronhatch.com

THERON **HATCH**

Made in the USA
Charleston, SC
27 February 2017